# The Art of Living in Relationship

Jorge Waxemberg

# The Art of Living in Relationship

Cafh Foundation, Inc.
New York, New York

*Originally published in 1991 as* El Arte de Vivir la Relación
*Cuadernos de Cultural Espiritual*
*Buenos Aires, Argentina*


*International Standard Book Number 0-9609102-1-2*
*Library of Congress Catalog Card Number 93-73655*


*Translation © 1994 by Cafh Foundation*
*2061 Broadway, New York, New York 10023*
*Printed in the United States of America*

# Contents

# Foreword

In 1970 when I first met Jorge Waxemberg, the spiritual director of the path of Cafh, I was a student, a mother of three children, and a disillusioned sixties radical struggling each day to fulfill the responsibilities I had committed myself to. Along with many others of my generation, I felt overwhelmed by a sense of pervasive hopelessness. We yearned to live meaningful, socially responsible lives, yet we lived under the heavy shadow of sorrow and loss of idealism that swept the United States at the end of the sixties.

We were filled with a desire to live with harmony and love yet had no oars to row the boat of peaceful transformation. We yearned to work together as companions in the struggle yet had little knowledge about how to relate to one another with honesty, respect and compassion. We longed for a new society, yet we saw daily evidence in our personal lives of failed agendas and self-destructive behavior.

Was it really possible to find happiness and realization and still live in ways that would be socially responsible and contribute to creating a better world for all—a just and peaceful society?

The challenge felt like an urgent calling in our lives. How could we, ordinary people, find a way to live that would make a difference not only in our own lives but in the lives of others?

Now, twenty-three years later, the answer I found at that crucial turning point in my life is still just as true, and there is still much work to do. Difficulties continue to exist, though in different forms; the yearning for meaning still guides my efforts.

I began to find answers through my inner work on the path of Cafh. By focusing on relationship as a primary part of my spiritual practice, I could learn to find purpose and authenticity in my own life and relationships as well as explore new and more harmonious ways of radiating a loving, positive energy to the world. I learned to begin with my own life, exploring ways to create harmonious relationships based on reverence and compassion. I could then apply what I learned to do at home to my understanding and sharing of the struggles of others—individuals, couples, families, even nations—as we all work to live together peacefully, respecting one another's differences and possibilities. Most importantly, I could discover the essential oneness, the Divinity, in every relationship.

Today many people are aware of the need for a deep inner work on relationship. This book helps us to see relationship in a new light. Have you ever before considered your relationship with yourself? With your problems and difficulties? With responsibility? With life itself? We learn through the marvelous pages of this book to see life as a great fabric of relationships of which each one of us has a part to weave. We are invited here to practice the art of living in relationship, to walk the path of spiritual life, a road that can profoundly change us and our world.

Señor Jorge, as he is affectionately called by his companions on the spiritual road, writes on this subject after many years of experience as a spiritual director of Cafh. People of all ages and backgrounds and from many parts of the world (North, South and Central America, Europe, Israel, Australia) continue to learn, from the beautiful spiritual practices of Cafh, ways of unfolding and harmonizing relationship in all aspects of their lives.

Señor Jorge has lived in a spiritual community of Cafh since the 1950s and has consecrated his entire life to the work of assisting others in discovering and fulfilling their highest spiritual possibilities.

To be with him is to have the living experience of a loving, expansive relationship. His humility, his attentiveness to the individual needs of each of his students, his joyful sense of humor, all contribute to encouraging those who have the honor of being with him to search within themselves for the strength and clarity to live according to their own highest vision of relationship.

His method of teaching is simple. He is the Teaching. He lives, in a nonassuming way, the ideas he writes about in this book. This is the way of Cafh—to live, to work, to be fully who we are in every moment of our daily lives, and to do that with deep joy, acceptance and gratitude.

It is to that journey that he invites us in these pages. Each step on the road is up to us. We find here ideas and tools for exploring the meaning of relationship in our lives. We come to see every relationship within its larger context, as part of an expanding spiral that connects us to one another, to everything and, most importantly, to the Divine.

I remember Señor Jorge's answer to a student who wanted to know how one could tell how close a person had gotten to God. He said, "Look at that person's relationship with other people."

Let us all use this wonderful book to come closer to God. Let us come closer to one another in reverent and compassionate relationships.

Judith Shepard Gomez
Santa Fe, New Mexico
June 1993

# Translator's Note

This text is the English translation of *El Arte de Vivir la Relación*, a book first published in South America as a selection of notes and guidelines for a course of study. In this English version, we have found it useful to expand the original text by adding examples and developing some of the concepts to make the text more accessible to general readers. It is our sincere hope that readers will find here ideas for daily living that will enrich their spiritual lives and make possible more expansive relationships—with their families, with their neighbors, with life, with God.

Patricia Colleran
General Editor, Cafh Foundation
New York, New York

# Introduction

This text has been prepared as working material for people who are genuinely interested in their spiritual unfolding. More than a book merely for reading, it is a guide for working on the system of relationships through which we understand ourselves and unfold our highest possibilities as human beings.

Who are we, really? Where did we come from? What is the meaning of our individual lives? These are perhaps the most fundamental questions, but when we try to answer them with words, we come up against the limitation of our human intellect. Working on relationships, however, is a way for us to respond, for relationships connect us with all aspects of reality, including those which we do not understand. When we work on relationships, we accept the challenge of answering questions we really don't know the answers to. Relationships, because they have to do with reality, offer us the means to expand our consciousness and to know ourselves.

Work on relationships requires that we have the daring to renounce the ideas we have formed regarding who we are, what we know, and what we want in life. It requires us to support ourselves on the task of relating harmoniously and consciously, continually expanding our view of reality while, at the same time, having the faith that, since we participate in all of existence, the final answers are indeed within ourselves. And we know this is possible: we see the inspiring examples of others who have already traversed this marvelous interior road.

In this text, you will notice that we sometimes use the word "soul" when referring to the human being. By "soul" we mean that which we have in common as human beings: our essential nature, our innate yearning to unfold our possibilities and to know God. Here, too, when reading the word "God," we hope that everyone can give the greatest possible amplitude to this word, without limiting it to positive or negative definitions. "God" and "the Divine" express the highest possibility of the human being and, as such, the point toward which we direct the unfolding of our consciousness.

Aside from our philosophical and religious beliefs, the concept of the Divine represents the unknown— that force in life and in the world which pulls us toward greater knowledge of ourselves and of reality.

The chapter on the relationship with one's spiritual director is dedicated to those who look for help in unfolding their total potential as human beings. We know there are not many true spiritual directors; nevertheless, those who fully accept the challenge of their unfolding will know how to find the guidance they need.

We hope that the work outlined in this text will help us actualize a harmonious relationship with ourselves, with all human beings and with the ineffable reality we call Life.

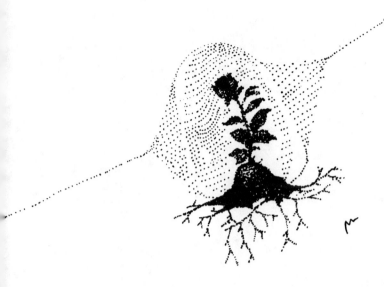

## Part 1

# LEARNING TO RELATE

 # Relationship and Spiritual Life

Spiritual life is essentially based on love, and our love depends on the character and level of our relationships. Relationships are the great fabric of life; to unfold them consciously and methodically is to learn to love through a work that includes all of life. It is to transform living into an art. Spiritual life and the art of living are, therefore, two ways of referring to the same thing.

Nevertheless, the term "spiritual life" is generally associated with a belief rather than with the task of living. When we refer to spiritual life, we need to remember that no one's life is autonomous or isolated. We live in relationship, not only with other persons and our immediate surroundings but with the world, with time and with the mystery of not knowing who we are, where we came from and where we are going. Most especially we need to remember that we live in relationship with the fundamental principle of the Universe, that which we call God or the Divine.

When we say that we want to be happy, that we yearn for fulfillment, we are actually expressing the human need to unveil the mystery of the Divine. We know that explanations of life and the world are not enough. We find real fulfillment and happiness only when the Divine becomes part of our self-awareness.

This realization is traditionally called "union with God." But the traditional definition does not include the fact that we are united with all of reality; we live in a great web of relationships that includes everything. If we were to think of the unfolding of the soul as a process that takes place only between the individual and the Divine, we would separate the human being from reality. Our relationship with others and with the world is not simply an arena where our spiritual transformation takes place. On the contrary, spiritual unfolding becomes possible when it is based on the harmonization of the relationship that we have with all human beings and with all aspects of life.

That is why the idea of relationship is so important to our spiritual realization. The human being is inseparable from the universe: we are and we live in relationships. Yet our relationship with the world is for the most part unknown to us; we are aware of only some of our relationships, especially those which we voluntarily choose.

We live in an environment that is as reduced or as ample as our consciousness. Our attitude, health, moods and the circumstances of the moment influence us, and the subjective dimension of our situation changes continually. Thus we may sometimes wish to relate with all human beings—our realm is the universe—while other times we do not want to have a relationship with anyone or anything—our realm is ourselves.

But we live in relationship whether we want to or not, whether we realize it or not. Nothing exists apart from us; everything exists along with us—it includes us. For a better society to be possible, we all need to learn to live together in harmonious relationships.

It would be good for those of us who yearn for a better society to look first at our own relationships and to put aside the belief that our originality and authenticity as individuals are expressed in an isolated, fixed or abstract way. This will help us perceive our individuality by the way we relate with the circumstances which actually include and shape who we are.

The spiritual tradition teaches the basic foundations of human relationships: not to kill others, cause others harm, humiliate others, or jeopardize their welfare. That is, we need to control ourselves enough not to cause injury. It also teaches practices that help us accept our neighbor: tolerance, patience, gentleness, compassion. Although these precepts show us the beginning of a basic human relationship, humankind as a whole does not yet live these principles. It is here, at these first steps, that we need to begin to become conscious of the character and level of our relationships in order to understand the task of harmonizing and universalizing them.

Spiritual practices lead to spiritual advancement only when they produce greater harmony in our system of relationships. To imagine that we are unfolding spiritually, while at the same time finding it hard to tolerate those we live with, would be to distort the meaning of unfolding. It would be a sad illusion if we thought we were on the road toward union with God if our behavior caused others to have to practice virtues to be able to live with us.

Effort is necessary to develop conscious and harmonious relationships. We need interior effort to work on the self-knowledge which will enable us to overcome the idea that we exist separated from others. We also need exterior control so that our conduct does not separate us from others but creates an unbreakable inner tie between ourselves and everyone else.

Although practices of self-knowledge such as meditation and ascetic exercises are recommended, they are not enough to produce real unfolding if our objective is limited to achieving a separate personal realization. To be able to know ourselves and to harmonize our relationships, we need to apply in our daily lives a universal vision that we glimpse in moments of introspection.

The union of the soul with God is also union with all souls and with all that exists. We cannot embrace the cosmos without including all of its parts—that which is pleasing and that which is not. To attain the infinite we cannot reject or ignore the things that seem limited to us.

The art of living spiritual life is based on love and is expressed in relationships. To love and to relate are the same thing; as our relationships become conscious, we become conscious of love. The quality of our relationships shows the nature of that love. When we relate consciously and harmoniously with our reality— which is everything—our love likewise expands and embraces all that is.

# Possessive Relationship and Participatory Relationship

Although the art of living in relationship is a process of continual growth, we could for the sake of discussion divide it into two major stages: possessive relationship and participatory relationship.

A possessive relationship creates dependence. The possessive person acts as if he can treat other people as though he were lord and master of everything around him, including other people, their lives, feelings and thoughts. When someone is in this state of consciousness and doesn't get what he wants, he reacts—he either becomes depressed or gets angry. The inevitable consequences of possessive relationships are pain and destruction.

Aggression in possessive relationships comes from the determination to dominate others. If one does not think of others as possessions, one is unable to vent one's passions on them. Although possessive relationships do not always manifest themselves in acts of physical violence, they always do violence to other people, to our surroundings, and to nature.

Possessive relationships undermine basic human freedom. Although someone in a possessive state of consciousness could conceive that others have a certain degree of freedom, in practice he does not recognize any rights save his own.

The struggle to dominate and obtain something through a relationship inevitably leads to deception and loneliness. Instead of uniting, the possessive relationship separates and, in the end, destroys that very relationship.

The vicious circle of possession and destruction is broken when we understand that our possessiveness hurts those we need to love, and we recognize the possibility of participation. This awakening moves us to put aside our instinctive and selfish impulses and to nourish our need to share, participate and offer ourselves to others.

We take the first steps in harmonizing our relationships when we widen our circle of love and learn to cherish others and to suffer for them.

To love more and more people, to work for the good of others without using them for our own advantage helps us to look beyond our own interests: this is how we discover everything that surrounds us and learn to respect it.

To respect is to relate with love, to allow room for people to express themselves, for nature to manifest its wonders. When we have respect, we discover the natural world which nourishes us, the life force in things that until now had no message for us. We discover the world of others. Through respect we become humble and learn how to learn: other people and even our surroundings become our instructors. We discover the teachings that we never saw before because of our desire that everyone and everything be subject to our will.

Through respect we begin to relate through participation. We change our way of responding to the circumstances of life and other human beings. Instead of reacting favorably to what we like and negatively to what we do not like, we learn to accept. Instead of finding enjoyment or suffering only when we are directly affected, we learn to participate in the joy and suffering of others. Instead of centering ourselves in our own concerns, we learn to enrich ourselves through the experiences of all human beings. In other words, we embrace all that exists with the same expansive love.

Relationship through participation is strengthened by appropriate practices. The basic work consists in creating an attitude of service by being attentive to other people's needs. It is not that we need extra time, money or possessions to help others. Everyone, in his or her place, has opportunities to help at the appropriate moment with understanding, words and especially with deeds. Simple acts (such as cleaning what we didn't get dirty, tidying a mess we did not make, sharing what we have and what we know, taking care of other people's things with the same or even more attention than we would with our own, helping someone else instead of doing something for ourselves, and watching the tone and intention of our words) are good ways to begin learning participation.

When we participate we do not give in to selfishness or thoughtlessness. We work continually on our minds and hearts to generate good thoughts and positive feelings. When we find that we are feeling sorry for ourselves, for example, we replace this feeling with compassion for those who have less than we do. When we notice that we are preoccupied with some trivial concern, we stop to remember those who suffer—the poor, the sick, the lonely. We remember that there is much to do to alleviate human suffering. These simple practices help us to see that we really carry the world, our surroundings, and other souls within our own hearts.

Relationship through participation teaches us to revere the Divine Principle that is present in everything. We begin to become conscious of our permanent relationship with the world and with all human beings.

# My Relationship with Myself

One of the cornerstones of the art of living is the capacity to know and to understand myself in the context of my surroundings. The first relationship that I must consider as I begin my spiritual unfolding is my relationship with myself.

As a human being, I do not express myself as a unity but as a composite. Genetic traits and acquired characteristics are continuously interacting and influencing each other. In their encounter with circumstances, they generate diverse emotions, feelings and thoughts that often are contradictory: altruism and selfishness, love and indifference.

I may believe that I am genuinely expressing myself, but the closer I look, the more I realize how little I resemble a human being with a coherent and harmonious demeanor; oftentimes, I am more like a body with many faces.

Sooner or later an identity crisis moves me to try to know who I really am. Thus begins a process of inner search for my real identity, a search that can be accelerated with the adoption of appropriate attitudes, standards of conduct and practices. Let's consider some of these possibilities in working on "my relationship with myself."

*To discover my place in relationship to others and the universe*

If I want to, I can shine by polishing my personality without recognizing my own littleness; but if I yearn to give a transcendent meaning to my life, I have no other choice but to universalize my experiences, finding my place within the great cosmic and human events with equilibrium and wisdom.

Only by disattaching from a self-centered life can I ever actualize my real possibilities. Discovering the life of the universe and the world of others gives me the necessary perspective to understand the extent of my possibilities and also gives me the strength to fulfill them.

I begin to establish a balanced relationship with myself when I understand the vastness of the universe, my smallness with respect to it and, at the same time, the extraordinary worth of my life as an expression of the same principle that sustains the universe. Until then, I fluctuate between extremes—feelings of grandeur and of personal insignificance.

No one is the center of the universe; we are not even more important than other aspects of reality. But each of us has a unique and irreplaceable place in the world.

Every one of us should be aware of the relevance of our lives to the whole of the society in which we unfold—to our families, our friends and all those who depend on us.

In other words, I remember my littleness in the cosmic realm and the importance of my experience in the nucleus in which I live. This leads to the next step of our inner work.

*To respect myself*

Even though no one is the center of the universe, each soul is an expression of the Divine. Therefore our lives need to express the reverence we have for the Divine within us. Although we know we are free to live as we wish, the consciousness we have of our spiritual potential does not permit us to live in just any way, throw ourselves into just any experience, or allow ourselves to be carried away by unconscious impulses. The possibility of expanding our consciousness to embrace all of reality is within us, and the way we live needs to reflect the dimension of that expansion.

Respect and reverence for the Divine presence within myself preside over the relationship I have with myself.

*To be honest with myself*

Self-respect leads me to see myself objectively, to be honest, to love truth above all things. Even so, we have such a strong ancestral attachment to ourselves that we unconsciously tend towards self-justification, self-pity and self-complacency. Everything that I think, feel and do is influenced by the strong desire I have to protect my self-image. To be truthful with myself, I need to transcend this tendency which is a product of the instinct of self-preservation.

To be honest with myself, I have to maintain a distance between myself and whatever happens to me, because only by applying certain means of self-knowledge can I make a more complete and impersonal evaluation. Time puts experiences in their proper perspective, and with it comes the necessary serenity to understand what has happened.

*Not to identify with the vicissitudes inherent in life and unfolding*

The more I identify with my experiences, the more likely I am to lose the capacity to understand what has occurred. Besides not distinguishing the difference between what I am and what has happened to me, I can get trapped in my mental and emotional states. I might have illusions about myself: my perceptions and evaluations are so subjective that I do not learn from my experiences as much as I could. When I identify with my experiences, I repeat them time and time again without understanding what is happening.

As long as we live hanging on to what has happened to us, we live for ourselves. We cannot see the points of view of others or their real needs. We don't realize that while we are looking at ourselves and thinking that nothing else is important except our own experiences, we are wasting the possibility of expanding our consciousness. Life slips through our fingers while we oscillate between feelings of irritation, elation or depression.

It does not help to get irritated when disagreeable things happen, because anger doesn't make mistakes go away or change reality. Mistakes are valuable when we use them to learn not to fall into the same errors and to maintain a spirit of humility.

It doesn't help to let ourselves be carried away when we are successful, because elation doesn't improve what has happened and wastes the energy we will need for taking the next step in unfolding. When we use our triumphs for reliving in our memory the feeling of superiority over others, we lose the fruit of those experiences. Successes are realizations when they help us advance, even though the next step appears difficult and uncertain.

It does not help to get depressed before difficulties, because depression doesn't solve the problems that make us sad nor does it make reality more bearable. We cannot expect life to consist of a series of pleasant events. Once we accept the sacrifice inherent in life, we overcome the ups and downs of difficult experiences and we live in peace.

I learn to relate to myself as a master relates to his disciple: accepting, teaching, correcting, encouraging, and always giving what is necessary for one to advance and maintain inner balance.

When I become conscious of my relationship with myself, I find my place as an inseparable part of the universe. I learn to respect myself, to be honest with myself and to recognize my individuality. In this way I establish a relationship between what I really know I am and what I sometimes believe myself to be when moved by emotions or unfounded ideas I have assimilated from others.

The more this relationship deepens, the more I learn not to become enclosed in myself. I respond to the need to expand my consciousness, and I learn how to give my life meaning.

# Standards of Conduct

As we learn to establish a relationship with ourselves, we become conscious of the standards of conduct we internalized in childhood. Such self-knowledge makes it possible for us to reinforce the standards that were effective and to work on those which were hindrances, so that we can build good relationships with our fellow human beings.

Standards of conduct have a decisive influence over relationships and it is good not to take them lightly, as if they were mere social conventions. Just as we need to speak the same language in order to understand one another, we also need standards of conduct that form a common basis of respect from which we can establish relationships. By walking the road of respect in relationships, we arrive imperceptibly at compassionate love.

Not everyone gives the necessary importance to standards of conduct, especially to manners. Although we cannot live without norms, sometimes we react against them. On the one hand, we don't want to control ourselves, but on the other, we don't want to suffer the consequences of another's lack of control. In the end, even the most rebellious among us have to subject themselves to at least a minimal level of standards so that we can live together with some degree of peace.

Acquiring good manners really is a necessary aspect of establishing standards of conduct. Even when we have good intentions, we often have problems in our relationships because we are not conscious of our inconsiderateness or rudeness. Even one instance of tactlessness can irreparably hurt a relationship. Good manners help us to overcome even the most difficult situations. They are irreplaceable assets in our work on relationship.

But we need to remember something: our standards of conduct will help us to unfold spiritually only when we follow them consistently. To reserve good behavior only for certain circumstances while allowing passions and instinctual impulses to go uncontrolled in our daily relationships would undermine our efforts to learn how to live. To be polite in public, for example, but rude and impatient at home cannot be our standard when we yearn to unfold our highest possibilities. We will find it very difficult to keep the spiritual ideal alive and conscious unless we work on one of the most concrete aspects of this ideal: to recognize the Divine principle in every human being. The way of expressing this recognition is to understand each person in his or her circumstances and to work to help everyone, without distinction. Just as we respect our vocation and way of realizing it, we also respect others' decisions and the way they are.

It is very helpful to be on guard against feelings of superiority and pride for they are damaging to our personal relationships. Although a person might mean well, he could confuse help and counsel with giving orders. As long as others follow his advice, he works hard for them, but as soon as they do not follow what he says, he begins to criticize them and wants nothing to do with them. This attitude causes many problems in relationships. It transforms everything into a fight in which one person tries to impose his or her will and opinions while showing disdain for those he or she supposedly wants to help. This attitude leads to bad feelings and resentment; it does not help others and, in fact, can demoralize them. When we are in this state of consciousness, we point out the mistakes and defects of others, forgetting to encourage and appreciate them.

Instead of asking, "What can others do for me?" I can ask, "How do I help others? In what ways can I offer my life, my work and my experience?" That is, we leave aside the attitude of being judgmental and we adopt the attitude of service. Others form part of our own lives.

In the end, good manners and clear judgment are really not enough for helping others. The effort to do good is all in vain if it is not accompanied by an unselfish love and a positive attitude.

Attitude is positive when it stimulates unfolding, inspires others and transmits love through advice which is practical, beneficial and possible to carry out.

A positive attitude supports and nourishes others, instills confidence in their capacity to unfold and gives them the courage to face their difficulties. A positive attitude also generates happy, healthy relationships, and this in itself is already a big help, especially in times of trials and discouragement.

A positive attitude is not a superficial optimism. On the contrary, it generates in us and in those around us the desire to make whatever effort is necessary and to work and sacrifice ourselves for noble causes.

A positive attitude does not depend on personal success and good luck. Pure faith in the Divine and compassionate love form the basis of a positive attitude.

For this reason, those who generate this attitude always behave in the same way, whether they are sad or happy, whether they are successful or not in their endeavors.

Even though it is not easy to express happiness when we are in the middle of a painful experience or to transmit energy and faith when going through troubles and illness, this is just what we are able to do when we live moved by compassionate love. When we see the immensity of the work that humanity has before it, we keep the sorrows of life to ourselves, transforming our pain, through love and sacrifice, into understanding and strength for all human beings.

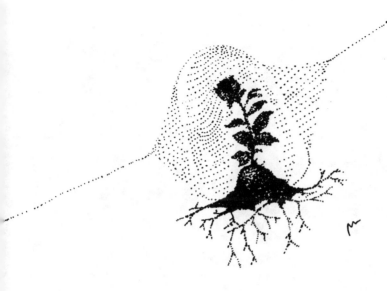

# Part 2

# WORKING WITHIN

# Our Relationship with Thoughts and Feelings

The art of living leads us to relate with our thoughts and feelings in an active and deliberate way. Instead of being at the mercy of our thoughts and feelings, we make a systematic effort to know and harmonize the way we think and feel.

Although our way of thinking and feeling is largely determined by heredity and the environment, no matter what our mental and physical environment may be, the quality of our thoughts and feelings depends on our level of consciousness.

The lower our level of consciousness, the more we identify with the mental currents around us and the more subject our mind is to impulses, passions and desires. In such situations, our life becomes determined by thoughts and feelings that we neither choose nor can control. We even defend them stubbornly without considering if they really reflect what we believe in and aspire to.

Human unfolding is marked by a long stage in which our thinking and feeling are determined by social conditioning and instincts. This inevitably results in ignorance, conflict and pain.

Even though there is a close connection between thoughts and feelings, our relationship with them is not always harmonious, especially when instinctive impulses and selfish thoughts move us to feel in a way opposite to the ideal that illumines us in the moments of our greatest understanding.

In general, the way we feel expands more slowly than the way we think. Selfishness and passion often dominate our understanding, and this of course is reflected in our behavior. For example, even though I understand that all human beings are equal, I may continue to feel identified with some people while rejecting others. My way of feeling does not match my understanding. Such an attitude not only can cause suffering to those around me, but it also has a negative effect on human relationships as a whole. To think in one way and to feel in another is an obstacle to the unfolding of consciousness and to building a world of peace and well-being for all.

We learn to improve our way of thinking and feeling by adopting a method of life. Systematic work on will and attention and the control of energy through useful intellectual activity and productive work constitute an asceticism for the mind and emotions that helps us achieve harmony. Feelings respond little by little to our emerging consciousness of what is good, and thoughts become subject to our will.

Besides following a method of life, we need to practice certain specific techniques to help us harmonize and develop the way we think and feel. Some of these techniques are surprisingly simple.

Let's consider this one: To attain mental control, we can make the practice of substituting noble thoughts and feelings for selfish ones. Although it is inevitable that undesirable, aggressive or selfish thoughts and feelings will arise sometimes, we can transmute them so that they will do good rather than cause harm. For example, when a negative thought appears, we observe it with as much dispassion as possible, until it is consumed by the weight of its own negative energy. We then produce the highest, most elevated thought we can at that moment, regaining control of our minds.

Let's imagine that we find ourselves having a critical thought about a person. As soon as we become aware of that thought, instead of giving in to our irritation, we generate a positive thought towards this very same person. We can say a prayer for him or imagine that he is surrounded by feelings of peace and love. We turn a moment of negative feelings into an opportunity to consciously produce positive thoughts and feelings. If we are consistent with this technique of substitution, we find that little by little we can change our negative reactions. Instead of wanting to wound others, we learn to respond with love.

Here is another technique for learning to control our minds: We make a practice of generating love for everything we have to do. Even with tasks that we usually do not like, we make the conscious resolution to feel love for the work, being present in the moment, feeling happy for the opportunity to do this particular job. This kind of attention helps the mind stay on its chosen task and, at the same time, helps us stay alert to everything that is happening around us. This practice leads to a heightened ability for attention and perception. By freeing ourselves from the incessant distraction of mental associations and unconscious impulses, we perceive what is actually happening. Every moment in life becomes a teaching.

These techniques are easy to apply, but for them to be really useful, we need to have a deep love for inner freedom. Only such a love can generate the strength we need for changing our way of thinking and feeling which defines us as limited personalities separated from the totality of life.

Right intention and continuous effort are, in the end, our best allies for attaining a harmonious relationship with our thoughts and feelings.

When we attain harmony between the mind and heart, we are free to think and feel in accordance with our ideal. We have within our reach the necessary means for building a world of peace and happiness for all humanity.

# Our Relationship with Shortcomings and Strengths

For didactic purposes, we can distinguish different aspects in ourselves: emotions, feelings, thoughts and desires. We call "shortcomings" those aspects that delay or impede unfolding. "Strengths," on the other hand, are the aspects that help us transcend our limitations and expand consciousness. From this point of view, our shortcomings are our field of work and our strengths are our tools for working in that field.

We are usually ashamed of our shortcomings and proud of our strengths. But we need to avoid getting entangled in this psychological game of identification with our various characteristics. We do need to work on our shortcomings because they are habits which foster ignorance. Likewise, we need to reinforce our strengths, because they activate the inner force necessary to know ourselves.

When we begin the road of unfolding, we discover the value of strengths and the harm caused by shortcomings. We are, however, conscious of only some—and not always the most fundamental—of our shortcomings. We may have shortcomings that are actually the other side of the coin of our supposed strengths. For example, working hard can cover ambition; disattachment may really be indifference; meticulousness can lead to intolerance; determination can hide conceit. By closely following our method of life, we are able to see our inner landscape clearly and ourselves objectively.

Sincerity, patience and perseverance form the basis of a good working relationship with our shortcomings.

When we relate to our shortcomings, we have to be careful to avoid extreme reactions. If we were to be constantly depressed by them and feel that all effort was hopeless, we would reveal an excessive preoccupation with ourselves as well as vanity for not accepting the fact that we are not perfect. And, just as it is not good to be constantly preoccupied with our shortcomings, neither should we deny them or ignore feedback from others when they point them out to us.

When we truly wish to cultivate the art of living, we learn to recognize our shortcomings, and we use them as a means of participating interiorly with all human beings, understanding that shortcomings are part of the human condition. As we work on transforming our own shortcomings, we develop that beautiful capacity of accepting others just as they are. Through our experience of working on our personal imperfections, we acquire the ability to help and accompany others in their efforts to understand themselves and overcome their shortcomings. Spiritual work on shortcomings transforms them into a means that leads to participation and spiritual unfolding.

Something interesting happens as we advance in the art of living—we become increasingly aware of our shortcomings. (As long as we remain ignorant, we find very little wrong with ourselves!) The more conscious we become, the more sincere we are when looking at ourselves. Frequently we become overwhelmed before the mountain of shortcomings that we discover and the few strengths we have to realize our ideal. In order not to get discouraged, it is useful to concentrate our work on one or two of our most counterproductive characteristics and to continue walking, step by step, stimulated by our small triumphs.

Although patience is fundamental for overcoming shortcomings, it is encouraging to know that we don't have to struggle with all of our shortcomings at the same time. A serious shortcoming generates many others that express themselves in different situations in life. To work on a specific shortcoming can help us to overcome other imperfections that at first glance might seem isolated. Selfishness, for example, can generate indifference, insensitivity, and impatience. When we work on our selfishness, we will imperceptibly begin to overcome indifference and other related shortcomings.

No matter how effectively we master our shortcomings, we can never think that we have overcome them completely; on the contrary, we have to always be alert and persevere in our effort to keep our tendencies under control so as not to repeat the same mistakes.

Humility and responsibility are the basis of our relationship with our strengths.

Humility reminds us that the desire to show off our strengths is really the shortcoming of wanting to be seen as superior to others. It would be counterproductive to use our good qualities to strengthen vanity. All human beings have good qualities; if we discover some in ourselves, we see them not as if they were exceptional virtues but as means for realizing our spiritual ideal. Strengths do not shine like jewels; in a harmonious state, nothing stands out from the whole.

Our relationship with our strengths should be based on responsibility, for we are all accountable for the way we use our good qualities, which are gifts. Virtue unites beings; it does not separate them into categories of better and worse.

Strengths are our point of support, the basis from which we unfold consciousness and assist humanity. When virtue is not cultivated, we lose one of our tools, and we waste the possibilities we could realize through it. A virtue as beautiful as patience, for example, could become indifference if we used it as a way to avoid being hurt by others or by circumstances. But well-cultivated patience is a positive way of responding to painful circumstances. Instead of reacting resentfully or becoming enclosed in ourselves, the virtue of patience makes it possible for us to learn and to accept. Patience enables us to love and to transform difficult circumstances into a means for radiating peace and helping others effectively.

When we take responsibility for our strengths, we become receptive and flexible, ready to change for the better, disposed to accept our shortcomings, and able to share our good qualities and gifts.

Spiritual work on shortcomings and strengths ends the dichotomy between the two and reveals that both are aspects of the same effort. The acceptance of shortcomings as inherent to the human condition transforms them into a means of participation, understanding and tolerance. Being aware that our strengths are our means of working protects us from pride and vanity. Being sincere in recognizing our imperfections is the force that gives impulse to our spiritual flight. And the humble acceptance of our good qualities reveals the potential that exists in all human beings, moving us to help others realize their highest possibilities.

# Our Relationship with Problems and Difficulties

Our lives often seem like a steep and rugged road which at certain points is very hard to climb. To keep this difficult road from becoming something so arduous that it is impassable, we need to learn to distinguish the difficulties that are inevitable in life from the problems they give rise to.

Difficulties are part of life. They are the moments which require our best effort and attention. No one is free from difficulties: all of us have to struggle to make a living, are subject to accidents, illness, and natural catastrophes, experience the limitations of our society, undergo physical decline and death. Difficulties, in fact, show us the obstacles we have to overcome to continue unfolding.

Problems, by contrast, are created by ourselves when we do not know how to face life's difficulties.

It is not hard to tell the difference between a difficulty and a problem. We know by observing our attitude. We accept a difficulty as a challenge and we are quick to respond to it. We understand that what we are undergoing is part of life, and we look within ourselves for resources to help us overcome the difficult situation. We also understand the need for advice, and we look for it with an open attitude, willing to work on ourselves.

However, when we have a problem, we will notice we have a different attitude. We tend to blame others, to look for solutions outside of ourselves. On top of that, we ignore the advice of those who try to help us see our situation from another point of view and find the strength we will need to overcome the situation.

When we have a problem, we want to stop suffering. But what we really want is for someone or something else to change, believing this will eliminate the cause of our suffering. Very seldom can we change the circumstances of life or other people. Anxiety and reactions won't help us solve the problem and in fact create an even bigger problem by adding distress and confusion to our situation.

Often a problem is caused by the attitude of thinking that we can gain something without making any effort. We tend to want all without having to work for it. It is easy to make an effort as long as we have enthusiasm; but when enthusiasm wanes, we are likely to think that life is hard and unfair, and we get depressed. This attitude transforms any regular difficulty into an insolvable problem, because we can never have our wish, which is not to have to make an effort.

Difficulties are part of life. None of us escapes from them. But we can avoid the problems that we ourselves generate with our attitude. Too often, we transform the difficulties having to do with the passage of time into problems. All of us get older, and the difficulties that come with advancing years are natural and evident to whomever is willing to see them. But when we do not want to face the realities of aging, we think the solution is to pretend that we are not really growing old, or that we will somehow be different from everyone else and not have to suffer the inconveniences of old age. We might even allow the passing years to become a source of fear and resentment. When we look for ways not to face our lot, very serious problems arise.

It is obvious that some situations do not have a solution, that the only way to overcome difficulties is to face them and work on them. Not to accept the roughness of the road is to not accept the road. If we do not accept difficulties, it is the same as not accepting life.

When we recognize that we have problems, we know what our relationship with them has to be: we face our problems with determination and energy.

The only way out is to learn the nature of our problems and the role our attitude plays in them. It doesn't help to know if we really have a reason for complaining, or if someone or something else is responsible for our situation. We will not solve our problems by punishing a culprit or by trying to change what is not in our power to change. It is only by working on ourselves that we can overcome our problems. We have the power within to change, to do better, to understand and to live fully.

When we discover our inner strength and understand that the origin of our conflicts is in our attitude, our problems are simplified. They become merely the difficulties that go with life. As we unfold the capacity to understand our attitude, we inevitably find the right advice, the necessary help and the inner strength to overcome our difficulties.

We learn to relate to difficulties with humility, simplicity and courage.

We relate to difficulties with humility when we understand and accept our limitations, when we come to recognize how few of the events of life we can control, and accept the rest as challenges for extracting the teaching they hold. We know that the law of life cannot be changed to our liking, that the only life we can lead is our own and that the difficulties we encounter are points of support for our inner work.

When we are humble, we can foresee difficulties, for by looking at life without arrogance we see clearly the road that lies ahead.

We relate to difficulties with simplicity when we love truth more than we love the image we have of ourselves.

When we yearn to know ourselves we do not speculate about difficulties. We know that difficulties signify work and effort, and we do not use them to feel sorry for ourselves or to justify an attitude of defeat. We look at ourselves just as we are, with strengths and shortcomings, with limitations and possibilities. We look to our future with equanimity.

We relate to difficulties with courage when we do not want to spare any effort to overcome them. We know we have the strength to live our lives fully, and we work with all our energy for the good of our soul and all souls.

When we discover that the secret of our strength is to be found in our attitude toward difficulties, we stop dreaming of an easy life and we get to work walking our road of unfolding resolutely to the end.

# Our Relationship with the Body

Reference to the body as something separate from ourselves is an arbitrary distinction, but it helps us to set up a dichotomy and therefore a relationship with the body. We are better able to decide how we will care for it, what we will do with it and even how we will understand it. A constructive relationship with the body is based on self-control and responsibility.

All of us are responsible for our energy, and we are responsible both to ourselves and to society for the way we use it. The reserve of energy is not, however, an end in itself. It would not do much good to gain greater control over the body if later we did not use well the energy that we had generated with that control. Knowing what to do with our energy is just as important as learning how to reserve it. The reserve of energy must be transformed into something good, both for ourselves and for society.

We have a personal responsibility with the body because the body's usefulness is significantly curtailed if we do not pay attention to our habits, especially diet, exercise and rest. Everyone is responsible for making sure that his or her body yields as much as it is capable of.

Responsibility has a social dimension as well, because what we do with our bodies affects society.

We don't always recognize this, for we tend to think of ourselves and our bodies as separate and isolated from everything else. But we can see that if we use the body sensibly, we can contribute to society. We will be strong and able and productive. If instead we are busy satisfying all our desires and following impulses indiscriminately, without taking into account the effect of such behavior on the body, we take unnecessary risks.

We cannot think we are socially responsible if we drive too fast and risk an accident. If we have a serious accident, someone else will then have to take care of us; we won't be able to contribute our energy in the same way we could if we had not hurt ourselves. We are not socially responsible if we risk contracting chronic or disabling diseases because of our behavior. Sooner or later we would become a burden on others, and they would have to spend their time and energy taking care of us.

We always have to assume responsibility for our bodies. Even those who consecrate their lives to doing good works are not dispensed from this obligation. We still have to make sure the body is well cared for. Helping others is praiseworthy, but is no excuse for a lack of self-control or attention to overcome those habits that lead to preventable pain and disability. What we offer to others would be taken back with interest if our bodies became prematurely sick or disabled due to imprudence on our part. It could even happen that institutions and other people would have to take care of our bodies for years, until we die, because of our behavior.

Mother Teresa of Calcutta realized our social responsibility for the body early in her work with the dying and the destitute. At first she thought that her nuns, who dedicate their lives to the poorest of the poor, should eat only what the poor eat: a meager bowl of rice everyday. She soon realized that if they continued that way, they would not have the strength to carry out their mission, that they would get sick and die young. She revised her plans and wisely ensured a balanced, nutritional, simple diet for the Missionaries of Charity, enabling them to use their energy to the utmost.

Control enables us to reserve our energy. Mastery over the passions and control over the tendency for self-complacency give human beings the necessary store of energy to unfold. Laziness leads to the pursuit of excessive comfort and to lack of control of bodily expressions. Gluttony is a distortion of the need for nourishment. Sexual and aggressive impulses are unconscious expressions of the instinct of self-preservation. When we master the instincts, we are able to distinguish clearly our possibilities and discern our real options in life.

To establish a relationship with the body, the first two barriers we have to overcome are an exaggerated preoccupation with it and the fear of physical suffering. The body is an instrument of the soul; it is not the soul who should place herself at the service of the body. An indulged body compels us to subordinate ourselves to it and to be dependent on its sensations. Moreover, the fear of suffering lowers our physical resistance and tolerance for discomfort and pain. But when we treat the body as an instrument, giving it the care it needs without indulging or debilitating it, we develop inner strength and become less susceptible to suffering.

We maintain good health by placing limits on desires that go beyond what is necessary and sensible for good health. An overindulged body becomes a tyrant. But if we look after the body and train it to work and be productive, we find it is an efficient tool for our inner unfolding.

We really don't need extra time or special equipment to take care of our bodies. We do need sensible self-discipline and the knowledge necessary so that our reason rules our impulses. Then we have the self-control to keep the body flexible, healthy and useful.

Sensible self-discipline in taking care of the body prevents us from falling into the extremes of neglecting the body or making it the center of our attention.

We do need knowledge. It is very helpful to be informed about the latest scientific information regarding diet, exercise and preventive measures in health care. Knowledge enables us to respond to the body's real needs and to avoid accidents and sicknesses caused by ignorance.

Even when we take the appropriate measures, there will be times when the body gets sick. We must then accept the experience, use it to our spiritual advantage, and do whatever is possible to cure our illness.

Many times we suffer greatly for what are just ordinary things: another birthday, more grey hair, a minor ailment or physical inconvenience. Wanting to stop that suffering, we cannot help but wonder: "I have everything I really need. Why, then, am I so upset?"

In such cases it is good to find out how much we are identified with our bodies. We might be reducing our whole vision of life to what we expect from the body; we may feel superior or inferior depending on whether we think our bodies are beautiful or ugly; we may feel useful or worthless according to the way our bodies respond to our desires; we may also judge others according to their physical characteristics. All this brings suffering and confusion. When the impulse to self-satisfaction triumphs over real love, loneliness and emptiness grow in us, even when we "have everything."

Identification with the body conditions us to such an extent that we associate our personal value with our appearance and physical condition. Physical pleasures might even become more important to us than spiritual values, and the condition of our bodies more important than the state of our souls.

Identification with the body leads to an exaggerated preoccupation with youth and physical beauty. We see it in the media, on television, in magazines: to be successful is to be young and beautiful according to the standards of the latest fashion. While the body is developing and full of energy, we feel full of possibilities and aspirations. But as soon as the body gets sick, less fit, or older, we feel that our prospects are finished, and we might even become overwhelmed by despondency and sadness.

As long as we identify with the body, no one can help us feel better. We are the only ones who can change the focus of our lives.

The body goes through many changes over time, and in our relationship with those changes we find teachings for our spiritual unfolding.

The physical body grows, matures, declines and dies. Good management of our relationship with these changes teaches us to question and expand the goals we so actively pursue. Observing our own bodies change and grow old helps us to attain an understanding of the meaning of life and death and expand our lifelong objectives.

For physical deterioration not to seem like a tragedy, we need to develop some discernment. The fulfillment of material goals is not our only end; we have to expand the significance of our experiences, understand our lives as a whole, and give meaning to them along their entire trajectory, at the end as well as the beginning. If we accept the law of life beforehand, if we get in the habit of controlling our passions and placing limits on our appetites, we will be ready to let younger people take our place when our bodies begin to decline. We will then be free to concentrate our energy on mental and spiritual work, without ceasing to make an effort to use the body well and keep it as agile as we can.

Control and responsibility in our relationship with the body help us to care for it with common sense, to keep a distance from material objectives, and to understand the transitory nature of exterior goods.

By not identifying with the body and treating it as a gift for which we are responsible, we learn to face death serenely. Not knowing when death will come moves us not to waste our time and to concentrate our energy on the realization of our ideal.

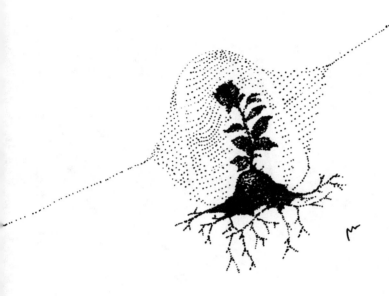

# Part 3

# EXPANDING LOVE

 # Our Relationship with Society

Our relationships with ourselves and with society are aspects of the same relationship, and they unfold simultaneously. As we travel the road of self-knowledge, discovering our identity, we also become conscious of the greater human society. We come to know that our relationship with society is to assume the responsibility we necessarily have because we participate in it.

Our relationship with society develops in stages that correspond to our degree of consciousness. It could be said that as long as we are enclosed within ourselves, we expect everything from society. Later, when we understand that our life is inseparable from humanity, we discover how to relate through participation. We then feel a responsibility to offer the best of ourselves for the good of all human beings.

As long as we pay attention only to our personal world and private interests, we have a vague and superficial idea of our relationship with society: we follow social norms only because we fear reprisal; we obey the law because it is the law. We live for ourselves, separating our lives and interests from those of the greater human society. In such a self-centered relationship, we establish alliances based on our own best interest. We turn to society only when we need it, and we take as much as we can from it. When society protects us, we call it "our" society.

Nevertheless, even though we call it "our" society, we don't really live in it. We prefer the comfortable little nest we have made for ourselves of our daily relationships. This is what we look to for warmth and reassurance, and this is what we really identify with.

But once we understand that living is an art that we need to cultivate, we develop an interest in knowing society and making it better. Yet, as we still tend to project our selfish interests over everything, we see only selfish interests in society, and we struggle to change at that level.

This is the stage of ambivalence; we define society as "our" society or "that" society according to the ups and downs of our circumstances, needs and states of mind. When society is "our" society, we identify with it and defend it. When we want "another" society, we attack it and rebel. We alternately defend, attack or ignore society, as if it were something outside of ourselves.

Society can neither be defended nor attacked. It is neither "our" society nor "that" society. Society simply reflects the process of human relationships; to attack or defend this process is to attack or defend ourselves. Such an attitude does not produce good results—it is based on ignorance that neither improves relationships nor makes us conscious of our attitudes.

Ignorance in our relationship with society leads to more problems than those that already exist and adds more sorrow to the tragedies that each of us endures.

It is not enough to say that we want a just society, without evil, without suffering. We can only build a better society by working on ourselves, making a concrete effort that results in good works.

We create a more harmonious society through our own transformation, because the more advanced we are in our unfolding, the more we know ourselves. We are more conscious and simpler in our relationship with society and better able to work for it.

Relationship through participation expresses the awareness that we are united with the greater human society and implies a constructive attitude toward our own transformation and toward active work for the good of society.

There are three basic aspects of relationship through participation:

- To abandon the illusion that we live a separate, personal life
- To experience first in ourselves the good we wish for humanity
- To accept and alleviate human suffering, creating constructive avenues of love and knowledge.

If we honestly want a better society, we realize that our lives really don't belong to us, that a life is something that must be offered to all of humanity. We begin to concretize this offering of life by reserving our energy. By not dispersing our strength in satisfying personal appetites, we turn that energy into the good work and helpful ideas which are needed at each moment.

Let us remember for a moment the life of Martin Luther King, Jr. Although he and his wife were both well-educated and could have lived comfortable lives in the relatively racially tolerant northern United States of the 1950s, they chose to live in the South. They knew they had to live, work and participate in the racial prejudice of segregation. Martin Luther King believed that he had to offer his life, his time and energy, to work for racial justice for blacks and, as his social vision expanded, for all oppressed people.

When human beings no longer have "their" lives, "their" objectives, "their" energy for using, they do not separate their sorrow from the sorrow of others, their possibilities from those of others, their vicissitudes from the changes that all human beings experience. They live what all human society lives, with all its contingencies.

When we desire to create a more harmonious society, we don't criticize, complain, escape, or look for privileges. We fulfill whatever is necessary, and when we discover something selfish in ourselves, we make the effort to transcend it. We know that we cannot ask others to do what we ourselves cannot or do not want to do. Therefore, we work to overcome in ourselves the separativity, indifference and selfishness that we see outside. This interior work inevitably expands to our surroundings and produces a chain reaction of good thoughts and good work.

We work for the good of society by transforming ourselves into beneficial cells that work quietly and persistently within the greater social body.

A constructive attitude toward society leads us to work in a productive and efficient manner.

Today there are large numbers of people who do not have even the basics for living, much less for unfolding their spiritual possibilities. How can we help them? By working efficiently: doing our own particular job very well, producing what society needs and consuming only what we really need. We learn not to waste: neither resources nor time nor energy. We work with attention, producing what is needed in the shortest time possible. We use the indispensable, and we do not accumulate excessive profits.

As we work on building our relationship with society, we will find ourselves having to face what we all come up against at some point in our lives: the dark side of human behavior. In society we see many manifestations of the negative side of human nature. Our instinctive reaction before the evil that others do is to want to defend ourselves, to attack, to try to eliminate the problem. But when we look at history we see that neither war nor suppression nor punishments have rid society of its evils. The only way to change society is to exchange what is counterproductive with something better, through understanding what has happened, through education and effort.

A constructive attitude toward society leads to the desire to learn and teach others. A good teacher first gets a good education. Then, as he teaches, he learns to adapt to his pupils, having special patience with those who have or create difficulties. The real teacher wants to educate all his students, even the ones with troubles. Likewise, we can create a constructive relationship with society by first changing ourselves, then working to help society, transforming its problems into opportunities, and building a better world for all.

We remember that education is not the same as indoctrination. To educate is to stimulate the process of developing consciousness. It is to teach to think, to discern, to choose; it is to reveal what ignorance has obscured. Our society is made up of human beings in the process of unfolding; the problems we have simply show us the deficiencies that we must correct, and this promotes the development of consciousness. That is to say, this is how we learn to relate with each other. When the social body is cured, there are no longer any symptoms.

The men and women who renounce to a personal life transform society by who they are, by their presence. They have no expectations from society; on the contrary, they feel indebted to humanity and offer their lives through interior and exterior work. They teach not only from pulpits and lecture halls; they teach with their very lives, fulfilling in themselves the ideal they wish to transmit.

Human beings who participate interiorly deepen their relationship with society through their reserve of energy, through work on themselves and in their active collaboration in good works for the welfare of humanity. In this way they embody the ideal of spiritual realization and place it within the reach of all human beings.

# Our Relationship with
# the Worldly Spirit

We often see the tendency in ourselves to live as if we were not going to die, as if pain and misery did not exist in this world, as if love were just another thing to be enjoyed without any need to cultivate it. The stubborn denial of evident reality, the blind impulse to chase after happiness without wanting to face the consequences of our choices, the banalization of love, is what we call in this text the "worldly spirit."

In all sectors of society we find the illusion of thinking it is possible to benefit without making an effort, to live without working, to have fun and no worries. The attraction of this illusion is so powerful that even a terrible tragedy does not always help us see the harm caused by such expectations—both to ourselves and to society as a whole.

We have to always be alert so as not to be carried away by this tendency to overlook the needs of others and pursue pleasure for ourselves alone. The worldly spirit is a force which always lies in wait. While a positive force moves each of us to actualize new possibilities, at the same time, the worldly spirit leads us toward inertia and negligence. It is something inherent in our human nature. It is as if we thought we had the right to indiscriminately enjoy the goods of the world without assuming any responsibility for it.

In our relationship with the worldly spirit, there is no compromise. Either we advance in the unfolding of consciousness and love, or we waste time and energy, slipping down the cliff of selfishness and unconsciousness. This is not a mere figure of speech: it can really happen in life. Spiritual unfolding is not a linear process that moves unfailingly upward; it is possible to get sidetracked and regress. If we drop our guard even slightly, the worldly spirit can take over and make us lose everything we had gained in our previous efforts to unfold.

Even when we have the best intentions, we have to be on guard against the worldly spirit, for it is not only in others that it exists. The worldly spirit has roots in inner attitudes and feeds on narrow thoughts, instinctual feelings and hasty actions. In other words, it feeds on that part of ourselves that does not want to recognize the spiritual dimension that life holds when we have generous feelings and noble thoughts and actions.

The worldly spirit can take subtle forms even in those experienced in spiritual practices.

It is easy to imagine that we transcend the worldly spirit by having an orderly, measured life, by working hard and being generally moderate in our habits. Certainly these habits are good, but a disciplined life by itself does not free us from the worldly spirit. We could be ascetic and worldly at the same time. If we have a selfish attitude, we could find self-satisfaction in the profits of a methodical work and the accumulated savings of frugal habits. We might live with sacrifice and measure for a time to later use our energy in self-gratification; then we repeat the cycle again, alternating times of responsibility and irresponsibility.

To overcome the worldly spirit, our exterior work of living with measure and fulfilling our obligations needs to be accompanied by an inner work and the amplification of our objectives. This inner work has two aspects. On the one hand, we need to observe our attitude with honesty, look at our tendencies and always choose the road of love. On the other hand, it is helpful to develop techniques to control our instinctual impulses with appropriate exercises, such as giving a larger scope to our objectives.

Gandhi had a simple practice that illustrates this idea very well. He wrote:

> *Whenever you are in doubt or when the Self becomes too much with you, try the following expedient: recall the face of the poorest and most helpless man you have ever seen and ask yourself if the step you contemplate is going to be of any use to him. Then you will find your doubts and your Self melting away.*

Our objectives are spiritualized when we put the good of others before our own benefit. Love for humanity directs our energy towards generous ends. Not even the moments of rest are outside our spiritual objectives. Sleep directs energy through relaxation and helps us regain strength and put thoughts in order. Moments of recreation become likewise as expansive. We enjoy activities that are enriching and help us to relax, but we do even more than that. Recreation is spiritualized when we live offering ourselves, because nothing is merely personal. When we are enjoying ourselves, we participate in the happiness and joys of people all around the world. We share, we communicate, we listen. We discover that we find happiness when we bring joy to others.

We remember that the struggle against the worldly spirit does not mean that we turn our backs on the satisfactions and joys of life. On the contrary, when we overcome the attraction of the worldly spirit, we find the plentitude that makes life simple, wholesome and productive. We learn from our difficulties no less than from our pleasant experiences, and we find joy in knowing that our own life is a factor that promotes human unfolding.

It is a good thing to remember that we are never free from the possibility of falling into the worldly spirit, because the tendency to dream of an easy, unconscious life is part of our human nature. In our relationship with the worldly spirit, we know our efforts to control it must be continuous. We have to work all our lives to learn to love ever more profoundly.

# Our Relationship with Responsibility

**E**ach human being is part of a universal system of relationships. All the aspects of our lives—our actions, thoughts, feelings—have an influence on our immediate reality, whether we perceive it or not. Gandhi, a poor, apparently frail human being, influenced the actions of millions of people simply by fasting. So great was the people's respect for him, that Hindus and Moslems alike stopped their fighting so that he would break his fast. We can see with his example how one individual can affect his surroundings in a positive way. On the other hand, the action of even one imprudent individual could cause a disaster. One irresponsible act could, for example, lead to an oil spill, causing contamination and an ecological catastrophe affecting families, industries, and immense areas of pristine land and waters. Although these cases are dramatic, they give an idea of the influence of individual actions on the whole world, both positive and negative.

The effects of our actions on our surroundings are not always obvious to us. In many cases, it is because of ignorance; in others it is indifference or even a deliberate decision on our part. Often we do not stop to analyze the consequences of our actions honestly or profoundly enough.

No action is inconsequential. If a chance happening such as the falling of a tree can change the course of a river, it is not hard to understand that individual actions, laden with the strength of intention and will, have an effect on society and the environment.

Although from the spiritual viewpoint each of us is responsible for our influence on the world, the way we understand and accept that responsibility depends on our spiritual unfolding.

People assume responsibility gradually. When we were little, we could not even take care of ourselves. As we grew, we gradually began taking on responsibilities: we had to put away our toys, help set the table, take out the trash. By the time we were adults, society expected us to take charge of our own lives and to look after our families.

Yet it is not society which determines the limits of human responsibility. We do, each of us individually: we can fail to meet society's least expectations or we can go far beyond what anyone could ask—even to the point of offering our lives for the good of humanity. It is we who decide.

In thinking about responsibility, we can identify three aspects: individual, social and spiritual.

Individual responsibility defines what we do with our lives. Though much can be done to help another person, no one else can live that person's life or die that person's death. Each of us receives the fruits, sweet or bitter, of our decisions and even our indecision. It is, in the end, I who live my experiences, fulfill (or not) my possibilities, and determine my destiny.

More specifically, individual responsibility implies that we produce at least what we consume, that we use our time and energy with discernment, and that we respond for the things we receive.

Since the sense of individual responsibility is very subjective, it leaves room for interpretations which many times do not really meet society's needs. Here we will identify two ways of interpreting responsibility which create problems in our unfolding and in that of society: sporadic responsibility and the misuse of one's social heritage.

Sporadic responsibility leads individuals to reduce responsibility to a few external obligations and to believe they are free to act as they like outside those obligations, even in an obviously irresponsible way. For example, someone may be responsible at work and negligent in his private life; as long as he is married, he may take care of his children but after divorce he ignores them; someone else might overwhelm her children with extreme protectiveness and neglect her elderly parents.

A sporadic sense of responsibility is also expressed in aspects which seem secondary but which still have a great influence in individuals' lives. For example, our daily interchanges with others greatly influence our day-to-day lives. We might be courteous with some people and uncontrolled with others; correct at a social gathering but imprudent and aggressive behind the steering wheel; careful with our own belongings and careless with what belongs to others. It is obvious that this way of understanding individual responsibility creates countless conflicts and makes relationships difficult.

The other common interpretation of our relationship with society has to do with how we use all we receive from others. Our social heritage is an incredible gift. All too often we do not recognize what we owe to society for all that we have received. This is particularly unjustifiable in those of us who have received an excellent education and are trained to fulfill a meaningful role in life, yet do not assume the responsibility expected from someone who has received so much. We might be good at pointing out all that should be done to have a better world, but in practice we behave selfishly or unwisely. It could even come to the point where other people have to take care of our needs and solve the problems created by our lack of discernment.

Simply by virtue of living in society, we enjoy the benefits brought about by the effort of countless individuals who have worked to enrich humankind throughout history with their contributions. The spiritual tradition, accumulated knowledge, technology, and material progress are goods that each person receives for the asking. This implies an unavoidable individual responsibility.

Each human being has the right to enjoy the heritage of society, but that right goes hand in hand with the obligation of enriching and increasing it.

When we assume responsibility for society, we feel moved to commit ourselves to the improvement of our society. We strive to produce more than we need, so that we can contribute to supporting those who are not in a condition to be self-sufficient: children, the ill, the elderly, the homeless. Even if we do not consider ourselves exceptionally gifted, our capacity for work increases to the extent that our sense of "being in society" expands, since love and interest multiply our personal effectiveness.

For society to function harmoniously, we each need to share not only material goods but also our talent. Society needs the gifts of all its members. The capacity to create, to discover possibilities where others do not see them, to multiply the output of resources will benefit everyone. No one doubts that the discovery of a cure for an illness should be shared. Just as the scientist who discovers a medicine places it at the service of all, each of us offers the fruits of our personal gifts, whatever they may be.

The great physicists, Pierre and Marie Curie, had this sense of social responsibility. After they discovered radium, a previously unknown element, it became apparent that radiation could be used in the treatment of certain cancers. Even though business-minded individuals wanted to market radium, the Curies, who were so short of funds that they did not even have a real laboratory, rejected the possibility of making a profit from their discovery. When considering whether or not they should sell their discovery, Madame Curie told her husband: "If our discovery has a commercial future, that is an accident. Radium is going to be used in treating disease. It seems impossible to me to profit by that." They made their research public, to the benefit of countless individuals.

Sometimes, though, a person's sense of responsibility can become misdirected as a result of excessive zeal. Many generous, hard-working people—parents, teachers, preachers—feel responsible for those who, according to their opinions or beliefs, are misguided or spiritually lost. These persons sometimes give beautiful examples of sacrifice, thoroughly devoting themselves to promoting social change or to preaching and converting. Yet believing it is one's duty to force someone to live in a certain way or accept a certain idea is not a helpful way of understanding social responsibility. It does not recognize the soul's freedom.

There cannot be social responsibility without respect for free will.

The third aspect of responsibility is the spiritual aspect; in other words, it is responsibility for human destiny.

As we unfold spiritually, the moment comes when we must accept responsibility. We no longer stop at the mere fulfillment of our duties, but we accept new and growing responsibilities toward ourselves, society and human destiny. Many times people assume responsibilities out of ambition and vanity. How much more we can accomplish out of love!

Our yearning to attain real love expands our inner vision and broadens our responsibility, moving us to give more and more of ourselves: to be better, to console, to participate. We continually live our ideal, which expands, like a horizon that is continuously moving forward as we advance toward it.

We begin to fulfill our spiritual responsibility when we are responsible not only for our actions, but also for the inner attitude which nourishes our feelings and thoughts.

We expand our thoughts and feelings by exchanging the instinctive habit of defensiveness and aggression for a habit of understanding, love and participation.

Spiritual responsibility completes our road: we depart from a state of consciousness in which we see only ourselves and in which our sense of individual responsibility is limited to our own personal interests. Little by little, through our experiences and our effort to relate and communicate, we begin to leave our selfish enclosure and to include society among our concerns. This expansion allows us to see the insignificance of our ordinary set of problems within the circle of collective suffering. We learn to see that our selfishness could undo all our good work: on the one hand, we work for others, but on the other, our separativity still produces misunderstanding and pain.

We come to realize that we cannot solve outside what we have not overcome in our own lives. This awakening represents an immense step in our unfolding. We know that it is not enough to try to create a better world if we do not overcome the selfishness which causes such misery in life; it is not enough to wish for wars and violence to end if we don't put an end to the turmoil within ourselves; that there is no union among human beings as long as there is separativity in our hearts.

In assuming spiritual responsibility, we return to our point of departure: our interior. But this time our vision and attitude have completely changed. At the beginning of our pilgrimage our inner world was a refuge of self-concern; now it is our field of work, where we learn how to participate and to love. Our total sense of responsibility expands our consciousness and our spiritual work becomes integrated. We learn to actualize in our lives what we hope for the world. Our exterior work reflects our inner participation, and our efforts give noble and lasting results to the world.

# Our Relationship with Life

We relate to life through our experiences. The more conscious this relationship is, the better we understand ourselves and our experiences. But when our relationships exist at the level of unconscious or instinctive reactions, we don't understand what happens to us, and we don't learn from life.

The type of relationship that we establish with our experiences determines the dimension we give our lives. Life can be a matter of simply enduring whatever happens to us, or else it can be an opportunity to learn, to unfold, to expand our possibilities.

We understand the significance of our experiences depending on the degree of consciousness we have acquired, so in order to deepen our relationship with life, we need to expand our state of consciousness. That is, we have to constantly redefine the meaning of life until our definition encompasses all of reality.

When the expression "my life" is reduced to what happens inside the small nucleus of my personal interests, my relationship to life is limited to my particular circumstances. When "my life" includes the society in which I live, my relationship to life expands to include that society. When "my life" is all the reality human beings can comprehend with their consciousness, my relationship with life embraces all of humanity and the entire universe.

But let's put all this in practical terms: what difference does it make whether I define "my life" in one way or another?

As long as our view of life is reduced to our personal circumstances, we identify with the things that happen to us: we fear the future, we hold on tightly to our possessions, and we suffer in our ignorance. When experiences cause us to suffer, our relationship with life might become bitter, resentful and pessimistic. Yet, when we do succeed at something or we experience an unexpected happy change, even for a moment, we might feel that life is wonderful and full of significance. When others suffer, it matters to us only to the extent that it affects us personally. We see the evils of the world as something foreign, outside of ourselves, "out there." The problems that come from natural causes or which all human beings endure become personal tragedies when they happen to us. Misfortune takes us by surprise and makes us think life is meaningless.

Even when we are not suffering from anything in particular, when we have all we could ever need, we might still think that our lives are meaningless. Self-enclosed as we are, we do not know what to do with the blessings we have. Our idea of happiness is an illusion—we think that to be happy is to avoid the laws of life: not to have to face adversity, uncertainty, decline and death.

A harmonious relationship with life leads to a universal outlook which includes simultaneously the particular and the general, the personal and the whole span of reality. With such an outlook we are able to distinguish between the aspects of life that human will can control and those it cannot. When we have a conscious relationship with life, we learn to take what happens to us as a means of participation. This means that instead of interpreting something painful as a curse or something pleasant as a deserved privilege, we come to see the experiences of life as a means of sharing with all human beings. We accept each experience as an inseparable part of an event, which is, simultaneously, a universal, social, familial and personal happening. We place our painful experiences within the suffering of all humankind, and we discover happiness in what is good for everyone.

With this expansive relationship with our experiences, we learn a new way of facing our difficulties. We no longer react against life as being unjust, but remember that, like any other human being, we are subject to the uncertainty of the future, to deterioration and death. We also come to recognize that not everything we suffer is life's fault—many of our problems stem from our own behavior. In order not to repeat the same mistakes, we look to human history and to our own past, facing the consequences of our previous decisions and discerning the results of those we are about to make. This attitude brings peace, well-being and plenitude.

The direction we give our lives depends on our frame of reference. If we limit our world to our daily interests, we are disconnected from reality. We won't be able to understand our experiences or make decisions that take into account their effect on the whole. If, on the other hand, we see ourselves as an integral part of a whole, we change our attitude: instead of asking, we learn to give; instead of wanting to win, we act impartially; instead of wanting to possess more and more, we direct our energy to necessary and creative activities. We no longer want to control others; we work to master ourselves. We want to consciously integrate ourselves with the world and life through total participation.

There are virtues which help us to expand the definition of our relationship with life: humility, disattachment, participation and reverence.

Humility makes us conscious of our limitations, helping us to recognize that our view of reality is partial and temporary. We are open to learn from everything and everyone.

Disattachment makes us conscious of the temporality of an individual life. We know that when we have a great desire to possess, our relationship with life becomes a struggle against time, since nothing outside ourselves is permanent. Disattachment from the results of our efforts allows us to stop depending on what is external and transitory and to discover the eternity inherent in continuous becoming.

Participation makes us conscious of the human condition, helps us to extend the boundaries of the personal and to become one with the surrounding reality. This integrates the particular with the general and unifies life.

Reverence toward the things that transcend human understanding makes us conscious of our real possibilities. Reverence for the Divine keeps us open and permeable to the message of life, helping us to improve our interpretation of events and expand our view of reality.

To the extent that we harmonize the way we live our personal life with our global view of life, we gradually understand the stages of our lives and the teaching provided by both sorrow and happiness. We distinguish between fleeting moments of joy—the result of passing experiences—and lasting peace and happiness—which arise from understanding, acceptance and participation. Being aware of the message in each experience unifies our lives and leads us to the fulfillment of our spiritual ideal. Moreover, the integration of our individual lives with universal life awakens a sense of eternity.

The more harmonious our relationship with life is, the more profound is our understanding of its message until life, the Divine and our very selves are seen as a unity.

It is good to make a habit of remembering the aspects of life we usually overlook in daily life—for example, that everything is transitory. A pain is experienced, but it passes. A spiritual realization is without doubt a big step, but challenges remain. This exercise helps us to put our experiences in perspective. It shows us how to overcome sorrow and unmask the illusions that keep us from attaining our highest possibilities.

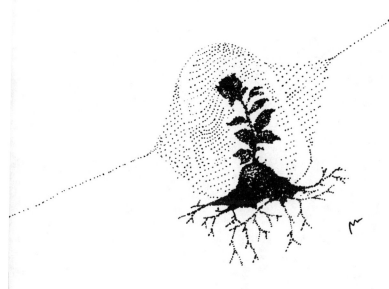

# Part 4

# ANSWERING THE CALL

# Our Relationship with Ideas

How do we find meaning in the events of our lives? What do our individual lives signify in our conception of the universe?

When we are searching for answers to the questions we face in life, we tend to look, first of all, to our previous experiences. We understand what is happening to us now in reference to what happened to us before.

Often, too, we look to our religious beliefs and those ideas we were taught when we were young. We try to understand what we are experiencing within the framework of what we learned about the nature of life, death, God and eternity.

Likewise, we look to history and to the ideas and interpretations that we have received from our culture—accumulated human knowledge, science and philosophy. The study of history and the sciences is fundamental for understanding the unfolding of human development and our part within it. Our vision of life is integral when it is incorporated into existing knowledge.

The interpretation that each of us makes of life determines what we do with our lives—it is the reference that we use to choose our goals and the way we will fulfill them. Thus, to have a universal perspective and to find meaning in life, we need to know how we relate with ideas.

Within the context of this chapter, we use the word "ideas" to mean those thoughts which are more elevated than our usual ones, those which promote our unfolding and enable us to participate with all aspects of reality.

In general, people tend to adopt a conceptual panorama through which they understand life and society. Our relationship with that panorama generally follows certain patterns that, to a great extent, indicate the degree to which each of us will be able to expand by means of our experiences.

Three types of relationship with ideas can be distinguished in this process: the emotional, the dogmatic-argumentative, and the relationship of silence-experimentation. These three patterns of relationship usually coexist in us in varying proportions. It could be said that we follow one or another of these three patterns of relationship depending on which one predominates in us.

When we relate emotionally with ideas, we are moved by concepts we believe to be true, but we do not really practice them. We imagine we are living these ideas because we are affected emotionally when we first hear about them, and we sincerely believe in them. But since we don't recognize any contradiction between what we believe and how we are living, we interpret our experiences in terms of our desires, according to our convenience, and we always find arguments to justify our behavior. We stubbornly defend our beliefs while, at the same time, we often deny them with our actions. In this state of consciousness, one could even come to the point of forgetting one's sacred principles: to love one's neighbor, to forgive, not to kill; justifying hatred and revenge.

In an emotional relationship, the reactions of attraction and rejection have a powerful influence on our interpretation of experiences and ideas. It is easy to generalize an opinion solely on what we like or don't like, labeling something as good or bad according to our own preference. As attraction and rejection form a large part of our upbringing and our habits, the emotional relationship with ideas also tends to be dogmatic.

A dogmatic relationship with ideas reduces our vision of life to a single point of view. We think our beliefs are the only truth and we do not accept any other. We might even project all that is wrong with society onto those who have opinions different from ours, thinking that they are the cause of all existing problems. Sadly, such an attitude is all-too-common in the world, evidenced by much separativity and hostility.

A dogmatic relationship with ideas causes conflicts and confrontations and, no matter how much one may argue, never leads to resolution or greater understanding. When we are all convinced of our own opinions, we are not seeking the truth. We want, instead, to prove that others are wrong. Here, of course, we are referring to a certain kind of arguing, not to those dialogues which produce an intellectual interchange, with each member really listening to different points of view.

An argumentative relationship with ideas is another aspect of dogmatism and, if we were at this level, we would tend to criticize everything that we hear. We would think we already knew everything, and we would hold on to the preestablished ideas we once adopted but never really analyzed. If new knowledge coincides with our ideas, we might readily accept it; if not, we would tend to argue about it and automatically reject it. Our dogmatic beliefs are like a prism through which we interpret life. All information is filtered through our belief system and serves to confirm our own vision of reality, supporting our certainty that we are always right.

We are not always conscious of our own dogmatism; interpretations are so limiting that they can make us believe our way of thinking is universal and that different approaches to reality do not even exist. As long as we have this attitude, we systematically reject all that does not agree with our ideas and we lose the possibility of expanding our way of thinking.

A different vision from our own is not necessarily mistaken, but simply another way of focusing the question. It is good to compare our opinions with those of others, not with the purpose of arguing for or against them, but so as to better understand our own position and that of other points of view.

The third kind of relationship with new points of view is that of silence-experimentation. In this relationship, we become open to new ideas, to different points of view. Our relationship with ideas goes beyond agreement versus rejection. Otherwise, instead of learning something new, we would see the context of those ideas only in opposition to our own fixed ideas. Rather, we now strive to learn something new.

It is not necessary to "believe" in new points of view, new concepts, new possibilities, even though they may open up new avenues of experience and knowledge. But we do need to consider and study them. The teachings that surround any experience give good results when we approach them as an investigator, open and free of prejudices. With silence-experimentation we learn to listen, to open up to a panorama wider than dogma. To listen and become informed without deciding beforehand what we will think is an excellent way to expand our understanding and to renew ourselves within.

When we discover an idea that is clearly useful, we need to look for a way to apply it in everyday life, so that it does not become just a passing idea. Even the simplest understanding requires an interior method of work if it is to become part of our lives. To practice what we learn for a while might be very satisfying; but to make that new understanding our way of being we need to maintain an attitude of observation, experimentation and fidelity. If we persevere in that effort, we begin to acquire wisdom.

An attitude of observation allows us to understand inner processes without distorting them with subjective interpretations. In this way we can identify what we need to change or improve and what concepts we need to apply in each case so our new understanding becomes a permanent conquest.

There are no set solutions for the challenges of life, nor are there fool-proof recipes to apply at each moment of human unfolding. The fundamental concepts of spiritual life have to be experienced by each person according to circumstances and individual characteristics. True spiritual principles are not in opposition to the results of analysis and experimentation. On the contrary, evident truths prove the validity of spiritual principles and these in turn teach us to use well the power that comes with knowledge.

To experiment is, first of all, to discern which concepts or points of view we need to explore in order to expand our horizons; second, to choose the way to apply those concepts in our lives; third, to evaluate the results obtained and, finally, to continue correcting and adapting our actions as needed to obtain the best results possible.

An attitude of openness protects us from the tendency to evaluate the consequences of our efforts as triumphs or failures. An undesirable outcome is not a failure but new knowledge which, if applied well, helps us to avoid making the same mistake again.

If we want ideas and experiences to really teach us, we have to always be ready to expand our point of view. Not all points of view are equally valid, since an impartial opinion is broader than a selfish one. To tell the difference between one and the other, we need to universalize the way we think and to learn how to resolve differences through continually expanding our interpretations.

We can, step by step, assimilate the teaching of life by maintaining an open and receptive attitude. Whoever wishes to cultivate the art of living is not waiting for a great teaching to come along, because life is like an open book. When we know how to read it, it shows us how to understand our experiences and to know ourselves.

 # Our Relationship with Vocation

Vocation is expressed through the meaning we give to our lives. We discover vocation when we ask ourselves the most fundamental questions in life: Who am I? Where did I come from? Where am I going? We not only ask these questions, but we search for real answers, beyond the ready-made responses of our times and society.

As we can see, this use of the word "vocation" does not fit the conventional definition. Here we are not referring to a natural inclination, capacity or aptitude. Aptitudes differ by kind and degree: people work easily in some areas and have difficulty in others. Very few people have the same aptitude for everything, and we tend to like to do what comes most easily. The more we work within our area of aptitude, the more skillful we become, and the more fulfilled. This might lead us to say that we have a vocation in this or that field—in art, for example, or science, mechanics or teaching.

But an aptitude for doing something is one thing while the capacity for unfolding integrally as a human being is quite another. A person might be superbly gifted for some activity and yet be a beginner at the art of living, not understanding his or her experiences or relationships.

Study and training enable us to work well in an occupation, but vocation implies the unfolding of all our human potential.

Vocation is not one more choice among an array of possible activities: it is what gives meaning to everything we do. It is what leads not only to the development of our abilities but also ourselves, as integral human beings.

People have different aptitudes—some of us are better at some things while others excel at things we cannot begin to do. Yet every one of us is capable of developing our consciousness. Every one has a potential vocation. We awaken to this vocation through a process of self-knowledge, which takes time and effort. Our vocation is actualized when we respond effectively to our need to expand our consciousness.

What, then, is our relationship with vocation?

Vocation is expressed in harmony—the harmony between our everyday affairs and the total meaning of our lives.

We can distinguish stages in our relationship with vocation: discovery, discernment and integration.

The first stage begins when we discover that living is an art. We realize that we do not have to follow the same roads others have taken. We can work on knowing ourselves and shape our destiny in relationship to a reality that transcends our immediate objectives. The interest in new ideas that awakens in us with the discovery of our vocation has nothing to do with personal ambition. It is moved by the desire to attain inner peace and better understanding and, especially, by the yearning to give meaning to our lives.

This step opens up a vast field of experimentation and discovery for us, but it also draws a dividing line between the interests of our daily lives and those of the new life we glimpse within ourselves: the material on one side, the spiritual on the other. Although we create a dualism with our attitude, in the beginning this is good: it gives us the strength of conviction to change our habits and direct our efforts to a more noble and transcendent end than that of self-satisfaction.

At the second stage we understand that there is no real contradiction between our ideal and our daily life. But we still do not know how to integrate the two opposing forces that move us: our true yearnings on the one hand and our instinctual nature on the other. Neither fixed ideas nor the euphoria we experienced when we first discovered our vocation are helpful supports. The only thing that sustains us now is our growing capacity to discern.

The stage of discernment is characterized by reflection and self-study. Vocation requires us to reexamine each and every one of our actions, feelings and thoughts and decide whether or not they further the fulfillment of our ideal.

At this stage we make sacrifices for our ideal, but we still do not love it above all things. In spite of our constant resolve to live with our eyes fixed on eternity, we are still easy prey to negative reactions and discouragement.

The art of living leads us to go against deeply rooted desires. For this reason, although spiritual vocation does not create difficulties, it does make evident precisely what we need to overcome to be able to unfold. In the measure in which we try to live according to our vocation, we discover more and more of those personal aspects that do not match our ideal. We might discover in ourselves, for example, aggressiveness, impatience or the tendency to argue, and we know that this is where we have to work if we are to unfold. When we find ourselves overreacting, we learn to pay attention to the process unleashing itself within us. Instead of wasting our energy in harmful outbursts, we can get to know ourselves better and work to transmute our energy. But, if we decide to close our eyes to our unfolding, we begin to think that our vocation is creating problems for us, taking up our time, interfering with our relationships.

Another aspect that appears after a time of inner work is the tendency to become discouraged, to go through what is known as aridity. Since work on ourselves becomes routine, we do not find the consolation that previously made things easier. On the contrary, the more we know ourselves, the more easily we discover painful aspects of life that we cannot eliminate or solve as we would like. Even though we are now able to discern our ideal, we still do not understand the nature of spiritual work; this is disheartening and makes us vacillate in our resolve.

This is a common experience for those on the spiritual path. Many great mystics knew it, and it is what St. John of the Cross called "the dark night of the soul."

But there is a light even in the darkness: after the painful period of doubt, we come to understand that hesitation is regression. We are no longer waiting for some miraculous intervention that will set us free. It is then that we decide to become totally responsible for our unfolding. And as we come to accept the designs of Providence, we enter the third stage of the fulfillment of our vocation: integration.

All the aspects of our lives come together in harmony through our single intention and our will being applied exclusively to what is good. The apparently disconnected pieces of reality begin to fit together until they reveal, in a simple manner, the perfection of the law of life. Our spiritual life and the task of living are one and the same thing. Love for freedom sustains our will, inspires our intellect, and nourishes our emotions. We become strong, resilient, daring, and brave—not because of our own virtue but from the strength of this love.

Vocation does not eliminate uncertainty or pain in this life, but it does teach us to live more wisely. Vocation enables us to face suffering, and even the most difficult of circumstances on earth produce the flowering of the best human possibilities.

At this stage we understand that fulfilling our vocation does not take away our time. On the contrary, time is multiplied because we learn to choose our priorities wisely, organizing our day harmoniously and sensibly. We increase our capacity to be where we are supposed to be, paying attention to what we are doing, generating at all times the feelings that awaken the noblest and most beneficial responses for everyone.

There is no final point in the fulfillment of one's vocation. We will not arrive at a moment in which we can say, "I have finished." Vocation refers to a way of life which develops the capacity to master oneself, to be at the service of all human beings, and to continuously expand one's consciousness.

If we make vocation the art of living, we are simple and natural, without aspirations to extraordinary accomplishments. We maintain a spontaneously friendly and productive relationship with all human beings, through which we transmit our peace and wisdom.

# Our Relationship with Spiritual Direction

All human beings need direction: in the home, in school, at work. Traditionally, we understand spiritual direction as the instruction or advice that is given to someone who wishes to live according to a particular creed. But in this text we amplify the concept of spiritual direction: it includes all the direction we need to be able to realize our real potential. We call the process of this realization, spiritual unfolding.

The work of spiritual unfolding is a task that requires wisdom as well as specific knowledge, and we receive this special help through a spiritual director. By a spiritual director we do not mean a master or a leader one must follow, because all of us have our own road. A director can help because he or she has walked the very same road that we yearn to traverse. The director brings his or her experience and understanding to us and gives us the support we need at each stage of our lives. A spiritual director does not require us to change our beliefs, but rather, helps us to expand our point of view, discern our vocation, recognize our path in life, and make use of the best means for traversing that path.

The very fact that we choose spiritual direction shows that we know what we are looking for and how we want to fulfill our objective. Spiritual direction helps us to always keep alive the election through which we have defined our life. In spiritual direction, both the spiritual director and the person receiving guidance have active roles. Both are companions on the road.

In reality, spiritual direction expresses our own inner voice in a particular moment when we are at the highest state of consciousness we can attain; it is the mirror we choose to look into to see ourselves in relationship to our ideal and discern our road of life. In practice, in spiritual direction we find someone who listens to us without judging, who counsels us without any ulterior motive, and who guides us in accordance with our own true yearnings.

The very fact that a person seeks spiritual direction means that he or she has decided to face his or her life. To say what we feel and what we yearn for is a way of clarifying our situation and our objectives for ourselves. Spiritual direction is the point of reference that we use to evaluate our subjective states, our advancement or stagnation, our choices and possibilities. The spiritual director helps us to be objective about our problems, discover our options, universalize our point of view and distinguish our own road within the complexity of daily circumstances.

Just as the physical body depends not only on the food it takes in but also on the way it assimilates it, our unfolding depends just as much on the spiritual direction we receive as on the way we live it.

The way we relate to vocation determines the effect spiritual direction will have in our lives. We need to clarify for ourselves the place vocation has in our lives, to what extent it prevails over other objectives, and how much we are ready to commit our effort, time, resources and possibilities to its fulfillment.

If vocation plays a secondary role in our lives, spiritual direction is a source of advice which may or may not apply, depending on our interests at the moment. But if we center our lives on vocation, spiritual direction is transformed into a fountain of counsel and brings us the knowledge necessary for our unfolding.

The result of spiritual direction depends in large measure on our discernment in understanding it, our effort in applying it, our trust in accepting it, and our commitment to receiving it. We benefit from spiritual direction insofar as we understand it. And spiritual direction is understood once we discern its nature.

Spiritual direction really is our own inner voice because the work of the spiritual director is to make clear and explicit what we really yearn for. To follow spiritual direction is to respond to our inner voice and to acquire the necessary strength to persevere in the realization of our ideal.

Spiritual direction is like a mirror where we can see ourselves in relationship to our ideal. The spiritual director's intention is to stimulate us to accomplish what we ourselves would like to be able to do. His or her guidance is based on the determination we have to work on our own unfolding. The spiritual director assists us in the elucidation of our choices and inspires us to follow our vocation. That is why spiritual direction would lose its meaning if we were to neglect our vocation or subordinate it to other objectives.

The guidance transmitted through spiritual direction responds to the needs and possibilities of each human being individually; it is the teaching a particular person requires at a particular moment. Therefore we are careful not to generalize the direction we receive. We need to discriminate between what is to be applied only at one stage of life and that which is always applicable. We know that the guidance we receive pertains to our own characteristics and is therefore appropriate for us and not necessarily for others.

The degree to which we understand the spiritual direction we receive is reflected in the way others react to our behavior. When we live spiritual direction with love and sensitivity, our conduct raises the level of our relationships with family, friends and associates, improves the environment in which we live and work, and rebounds positively on all society.

It can happen that we apply the guidance we receive in such a way that, instead of producing positive results, it generates reaction and resentment in others. For example, we might discipline our lives with great willpower and demand the same asceticism in those around us; our zeal might move us to treat harshly those we love but who do not think as we do. This, we can be sure, is not the way to help. We create a good influence on our environment not by trying to impose ourselves on others but by elevating our feelings and thoughts and, especially, by having a tolerant and compassionate attitude.

To be able to fulfill our vocation, we need to do more than understand the spiritual direction we receive: we have to make a permanent effort to put what we understand into practice.

We need to master our impulses and desires in order to direct our energy toward our chosen ideal. This implies being alert to all aspects of our conduct and gradually improving the way we respond to circumstances and events.

It could happen that we react negatively to the direction we receive with the excuse that we don't agree with it, when the real problem is that we don't have enough willpower to put it into practice.

Willpower develops to a remarkable degree when we make a continuous effort. Willpower helps us to meet life with a great feeling of inner security. We feel strong and free because we can choose how to react to circumstances, and we know we will act in the way we have decided to act.

Spiritual direction is based on the trust we place in the director we have chosen. Our spiritual director trusts in our attitude of reaching always for the highest good, and we in turn rest assured that our spiritual director will lead us steadily toward the realization of our ideal. Mutual trust enriches both the spiritual director and the soul, and transforms a relationship of apparent dependence into one of spiritual companionship, where two walk a road together.

At all moments we have to assume responsibility for our unfolding, for we are the ones who determine our lives and face the consequences of our choices and actions. Although the spiritual director offers us guidance and advice, we are responsible for our decisions. We do not do something because someone tells us to; we do it because we decide to.

Spiritual direction is not a panacea; it does not eliminate the difficulties of life but it does help us resolve our conflicts, avoid needless suffering, fulfill our highest possibilities and live our experiences in such a way that they result in our own good and the good of everyone.

By asking for guidance we express our decision to pledge our lives to the fulfillment of our vocation. By accepting to guide a soul, the spiritual director intertwines his or her life with that soul's life until the soul fulfills her ideal. Spiritual directors are not free, for their lives are determined by the needs of those who depend on them.

Spiritual direction places an enormous responsibility on the spiritual director. By seeking spiritual direction and assuming responsibility for our own unfolding, we are obliging the spiritual director to act impeccably, to conduct him or herself flawlessly. Inner preparation and continuous intellectual improvement are not enough; spiritual directors have to place their everyday personalities aside, along with their preferences and personal opinions. Only renouncement to him or herself allows the spiritual director to offer souls a transcendent teaching and the means they need to fulfill their spiritual possibilities.

When the spiritual director is before a soul, the director never forgets that his or her voice must express what the soul needs to hear. When we are before our spiritual director we never forget that the only thing we can hope for from him or her is the message of our own vocation.

# Our Relationship with God

The art of living teaches us that, if we improve our relationship with our neighbor, it is not to gain something but to be able to help more. If we improve our relationship with the earth, it is not to exploit it even more but to cooperate with it. If we look for a better relationship with the Divine, it is not to make sure we will go to heaven but to transcend the notion of being a separate and opposite entity; it is to become aware that we exist in participation and union with God.

From a spiritual point of view, relationship is a means and not an end. As can happen with any means, if our intention is not clear, we can lose sight of our real goal.

The end that we pursue in working on our relationships determines what we get: whether we try to use everything around us to our advantage, everything that we define as "not myself," or whether we work to attain the highest degree of love. For our work on improving our relationships to have a transcendent meaning, our intention, our aim, has to be union. For this reason, our work on relationships has to be understood as a means and respond clearly to two fundamental questions: Why do we work to harmonize relationships? And to what end do we work?

Why work to harmonize relationships? Because this work gives us the means to overcome separativity.

To what end do we work? We work to expand our consciousness through an increasingly more profound love; in other words, to attain union with God.

In the process of harmonizing our relationships, we advance through different degrees of participation marked by two stages of relationship with others and with God: (1) relationship directed toward survival and conquest and (2) relationship oriented toward participation.

When we talk about the first stage, we can look at it in terms of periods: competition, tolerance, and solidarity.

The long stage of the struggle for survival and the desire for conquest is based on the division we make between what we believe we are and what we think everything else is—other human beings, nature, the universe, God.

The need for survival leads us to compete at any cost, without considering the consequences, and makes of our relationship with God one in which we strive to assure that we will win existence as a separate entity in this world and in the next. God is supposed to protect us in this world from natural catastrophes, illnesses, and enemies; we expect Him to protect us after death in the other world as well. Since, at this stage of our relationship, we fear God's anger and punishment, we make offerings to God in exchange for His favors; we make a pact with God so that He will support us in our competition with our adversaries.

Even though today we as human beings have developed enough to be able to protect ourselves and to obtain what we need to survive, we might still maintain this competitive attitude. Thinking of oneself as something separate from the whole tends to lead one to try to manipulate everything and to destroy whatever interferes with what one desires. One might even compete unconsciously with the God one worships. But, in this stage of development, not knowing who we are or why we are alive, we humble ourselves and prostrate ourselves before God, asking for help and mercy. Our relationship with God is one of hope, on the one hand, and of resignation, on the other.

The suffering caused by this isolation eventually teaches us to measure the cost of competition and to value tolerance of others and acceptance of the will of God.

Tolerance leads gradually to solidarity, the most beautiful period of the first stage. Although division between ourselves and others still exists, compassion raises the level of the relationship. We not only tolerate others, we even collaborate with them, assist them in their needs and share what we have with them.

Solidarity is also shown in respect for the earth and its resources, concern for their use, and in the effort to repair the harm already done to the planet.

Solidarity opens the doors to participation with all souls and with God.

At the stage of participation, we know we are part of a whole and we feel it. We express this spontaneously through our relationships. Our response to the need for unfolding is at the same time a response to what is needed for the advancement of all of humankind. Our personal good and the good of humankind become one.

Even though we perceive only certain aspects of the system of relationships to which we belong, the fact that we participate in it implies that we have the possibility of being conscious of the whole system. Working on relationships makes this potential a reality and gradually unfolds our consciousness as we move toward a state of union with God.

Awareness that we are participating in the totality of life is a state we arrive at gradually through a long process which does not seem to have an end.

We establish relationships in our effort to connect with all aspects of life, but as our circle expands, the lines of relationship begin to fuse together. A moment comes when relationship is not "with" someone or "with" God, but everything acquires reality within us.

Union with God cannot be explained; it is a mystery that takes place in the innermost part of the soul. What we can observe is the gradual simplification of our relationships until they become integrated into a single relationship. We see that improving relationships does not mean more complexity and sophistication but is just the reverse: it leads to simplicity and transparency.

To deepen our relationship with God, we need the daring to renounce supports, the courage to leave the refuge of our preestablished ideas, and the determination to channel our efforts in a viable method that leads to our unfolding.

Working on our system of relationships is a basic part of this method. It is a work that can be done by all human beings, since relationships form the very fabric of life. To learn to relate is the same as to learn the art of living: when we harmonize and expand our system of relationships, we embrace the vastness of the universe. Our love covers everyone and everything. Our consciousness prepares itself to unveil the mystery of the Divine.

# APPENDIX

APPENDIX

## About Cafh

"Cafh" is an ancient word referring to the soul's yearning to know God. Its meaning implies the whole spectrum of the soul's spiritual unfolding, from the effort the soul makes to attain to God, to the divine grace she receives to assist her in that effort. Cafh as a spiritual path was founded in 1937 in Argentina by don Santiago Bovisio and expanded to Brazil, Chile and many other countries in the Americas. Chapters of Cafh are found today in the United States, Canada, Australia, Spain, France and Israel.

Cafh is not a large institution. Rather it consists of small groups of individuals who meet regularly and who share a common yearning to discover the meaning of life, to integrate that meaning into all aspects of daily experience and relationships. Cafh gives its members the gifts of a method of life, spiritual exercises such as meditation, and the individual assistance of spiritual direction. There are no fees to participate in Cafh. Love for humanity, the yearning to transform oneself and the willingness to undertake the task are the only requirements for walking the road of Cafh.

Cafh Foundation is a nonprofit organization founded in the United States to foster the ideals of Cafh and work for the spiritual development and welfare of all human beings. Besides publishing books on spiritual themes, Cafh Foundation publishes a quarterly journal, **Seeds of Unfolding**, devoted to the art of living. Cafh Foundation also sponsors conferences, retreats, courses of study, lectures, and dialogues on all aspects of spiritual life throughout the United States and Canada.

For further information regarding the activities of Cafh
Foundation, contact the address nearest you:

**Atlanta**
402 Theresa Court, N.W.
Tucker, GA  30084
(404) 564-9298

**Boston**
225 Walden Street
Cambridge, MA  02140
(617) 661-0608

**Chicago**
2627 Poplar Street
Evanston, IL  60201
(708) 866-6515

**Columbus**
7626 Perry Road
Delaware, OH  43015
(614) 548-6586

**Los Angeles**
475 Ladera Street
Monterey Park, CA  91754
(213) 264-7611

**Miami**
P.O. Box 653754
Miami, FL  33265
(305) 279-8604

**New York City**
2061 Broadway
New York, NY  10023
(212) 724-4260

**New York**
51 Cedar Lane
Ossining, NY  10562
(914) 762-8150

**San Francisco**  P.O. Box 4665
Berkeley, CA 94704
(510) 620-0222

**Santa Fe**  Rt. 9 Box 86 MB
Santa Fe, NM 87505
(505) 988-4321

**St. Louis**  750 N. Forest Avenue
St. Louis, MO 63119
(314) 469-1087

**Washington, DC**  P.O. Box 13291
Arlington, VA 22219
(703) 525-7974 or
(301) 441-3938

**Sydney,
Australia**  404-B Old Northern Road
Glenhaven, NSW 2154
(02) 899-6997

**Toronto,
Canada**  2254 Taylor's Orchard
Mississauga, Ontario L5B 2T3
(416) 276-2016

# On Community Life

The deepening of the character and level of our relationships is something that takes shape and unfolds in daily life. It is a process that develops over time, requiring effort and love. When people are committed to a spiritual ideal, this process of expanding relationships is greatly accelerated.

Since ancient times, many groups of people with spiritual ideals have come together to live and work in Community. We see the example of the monastic traditions of the West: the early communities of the Essenes, the Gnostics, the first monasteries of the Christians, the spiritual tradition of the Sufis. We see Community life in the East: the monastic orders of the Buddhists, the ashrams of the Hindus. In all times and in all cultures we find the aspiration of individuals to devote their lives to knowing God and loving ever better their fellow human beings.

The art of living in relationship is applicable to all: friends, families, neighbors, colleagues, and even for humankind as a whole. And it is given one of its best expressions in Community life, where all the members are committed to a spiritual ideal. For when all in a group have the yearning to unfold their highest possibilities, all help one another to fulfill their ideal.

Spiritual life is based on love, and love is expressed through our relationships—with one another, with the environment, with the Divine. Love is not an abstract concept: it is made real when people live together with understanding, acceptance, companionship and peace. Community life helps us to become conscious of the influence our relationships have on all aspects of our lives. Sorrow and pain, joy and peace, life and death acquire unfathomable depth when lived and understood within the framework of commitment to a spiritual ideal. Community life, as an expression of spiritual life, is the transformation of living into an art. It is to learn how to love ever more deeply—one's spiritual companions, one's relatives, one's environment, and all souls everywhere, known and unknown.

This foundation of work and love was the basis upon which the first Community of Cafh was founded in 1949. Since then, many more communities, some for men, others for women, have been formed throughout the Americas. Each Community is self-sufficient, and the exterior work of each ranges from schools for young children, to farms, factories, bakeries, and medical dispensaries.

The exterior work of the Community is an expression of its members' participation in the efforts and contributions made by human beings around the world who work for a living. The interior work of each Community member expresses the commitment to oneself, to the Divine, and to humanity as each one works within to expand all aspects of relationship.

Community life is the most-suitable means some members of Cafh have found to work for the advancement and well-being of humankind. To this noble task they devote their energy, their love, and their very lives.

NOTES